FISH

Elizabeth Clark

Illustrations by John Yates

Carolrhoda Books, Inc./Minneapolis

All words that appear in **bold** are
explained in the glossary on page 30

First published in the U.S. in 1990 by
Carolrhoda Books, Inc.

Copyright © 1989 Wayland (Publishers) Ltd., Hove, East
Sussex. First published 1989 by Wayland (Publishers) Ltd.

Library of Congress Cataloging-in-Publication Data

Clark, Elizabeth.
  Fish.

  Includes index.
  Summary: Discusses the role of fish in history and
describes how they are caught, processed, and prepared
for food.
  1. Fish as food—Juvenile literature. 2. Fisheries—
Juvenile literature. [1. Fish as food] I. Yates,
John, ill. II. Title.
TX385.C53   1990   641.3′92   89-489
ISBN 0-87614-376-1 (lib. bdg.)

Printed in Italy by G. Canale C.S.p.A., Turin
Bound in the United States of America

1 2 3 4 5 6 7 8 9 10 99 98 97 96 95 94 93 92 91 90 89

Contents

What are fish?

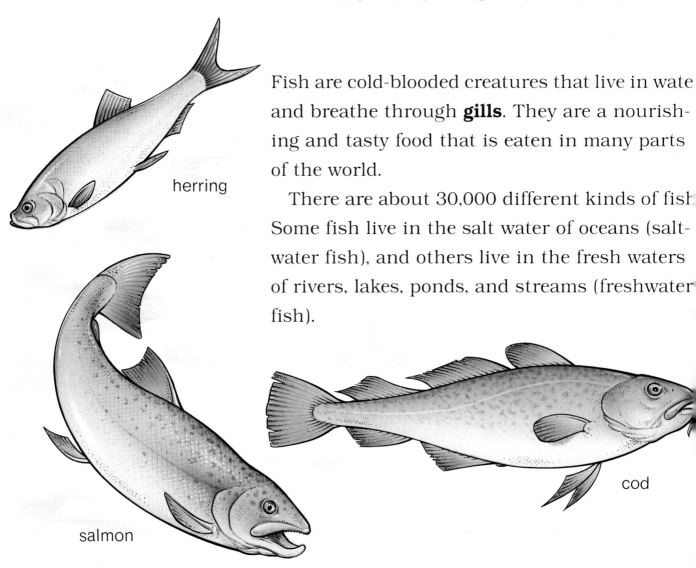

herring

Fish are cold-blooded creatures that live in wate and breathe through **gills**. They are a nourishing and tasty food that is eaten in many parts of the world.

There are about 30,000 different kinds of fish. Some fish live in the salt water of oceans (saltwater fish), and others live in the fresh waters of rivers, lakes, ponds, and streams (freshwater fish).

salmon

cod

Many different species of fish can be eaten, but only fish that can be caught in large numbers are important to the fishing industry. Every year, about 77 million tons of fish are caught in the world's fishing grounds, or **isheries**. Today, many countries have large ishing industries.

Some of the most widely caught saltwater ish are cod, herring, haddock, tuna, mackerel, lounder, and halibut. Trout, salmon, bass, and arp are among the most popular freshwater fish n North America.

shark

tuna

flounder

Fish in history

In some countries, people still use fishing methods that are centuries old. This Sri Lankan boy is fishing on a stilt.

People have caught and eaten fish since early times. Archaeologists have found nets, traps, fishing lines, and fish hooks dating from the Stone Age. The early Chinese spun silk fishing lines, and the ancient Egyptians wove fish nets using twine made from flax. The ancient Greeks made traps to catch tuna. At first, people fished standing on dry land or in shallow water. Eventually, however, they learned how to build boats which allowed them to fish in deeper waters. Gradually, fishing industries grew up in countries all over the world. The development of **trawlers** special fishing boats, meant that large numbers of fish could be caught at once.

Fish farming has a long history. Centuries ago people raised fish in ponds to make sure they always had a supply of fresh fish to eat. As early

s 3,000 B.C., fish were bred for food in salt-water pools in China. The Romans also bred ish in special ponds. In the Middle Ages, monks ept "stew ponds" stocked with carp for making ish stew.

These African children are fishing with traps that are similar to those used in the earliest times.

Fish as food

Fish is very good for us. It supplies many of the nutrients that our bodies need to stay healthy.

Fish contains about as much protein as meat. Protein helps us grow and gives us energy. Fish also contains fat, which provides energy and warmth. The fat in fish is better for our bodies

These Australian children have caught a big fish that will make a nutritious meal.

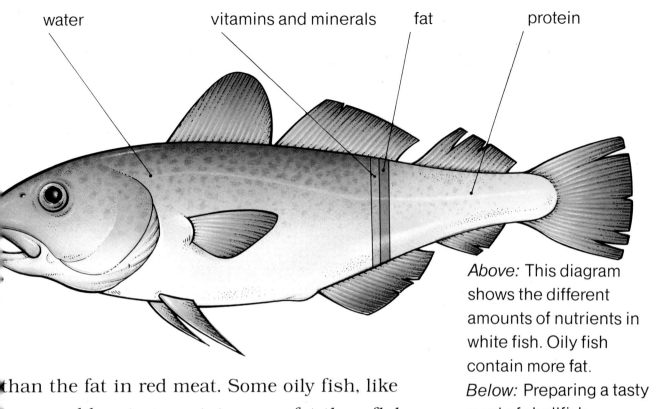

water · vitamins and minerals · fat · protein

Above: This diagram shows the different amounts of nutrients in white fish. Oily fish contain more fat.
Below: Preparing a tasty meal of shellfish

than the fat in red meat. Some oily fish, like tuna and herring, contain more fat than flaky white fish such as cod and flounder.

Fish is rich in vitamins and in minerals such as zinc, iodine, phosphorus, and potassium. These nutrients protect the body from disease and help it to function properly. The oils from the livers of certain fish are also rich in vitamins. Nutrition experts say that eating plenty of fish helps keep us healthy.

Saltwater fish

The seas and oceans teem with a huge variety of fish and sea creatures. Different forms of life in the sea feed off each other. Some fish eat other fish, worms, shellfish, or tiny animal **plankton**. Other fish are plant-eaters, feeding off plant

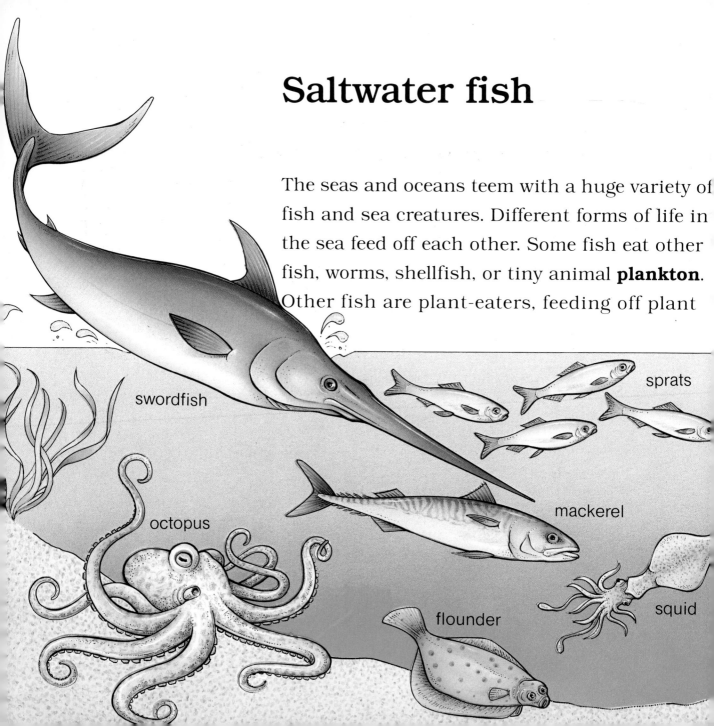

swordfish

sprats

octopus

mackerel

flounder

squid

plankton and algae.

Different species of fish live at different levels in the water. Tuna, herring, and sprats are among the types of fish that live close to the surface. Flatfish, such as flounder and halibut, live close to the ocean floor.

All kinds of vessels go out to sea to search for fish. They range from small wooden boats

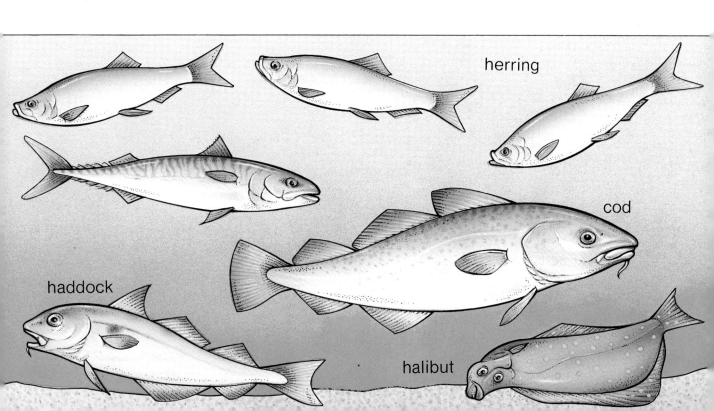

to huge commercial ships. Today, electronic devices called sonars use sound waves to make it easier for ships to find fish.

One method of catching fish that live close to the ocean floor is to scoop them up in a nylon trawl net, a huge, funnel-shaped net that is towed by a trawler and dragged along the ocean floor.

Fishermen selling their catch to a buyer at a port in Mexico

Right: An illustration of a purse-seine net

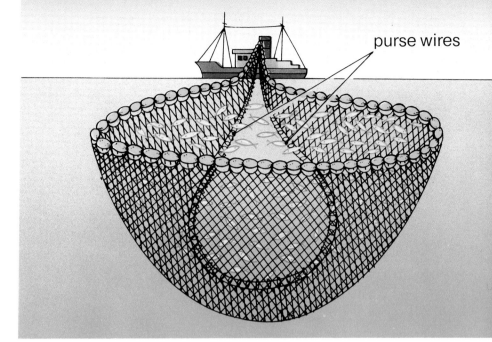

purse wires

Below: These Portuguese fishermen are unloading eels from the ship's hold for auction at the port.

To catch fish living near the surface of the water, **purse-seine nets** are most often used. These huge nets surround a school of fish like a giant lasso. The net is closed by pulling on lines at the bottom of the net, gathering it in like purse strings.

People have invented various other ways of catching fish. Stunning them with electric currents and sucking them out of the water with giant suction pumps are two such ways.

13

Fish in danger

Pollution is not only a danger to all sea creatures. It can also affect the livelihood of people such as this crab fisherman in Chile.

Today, fish are increasingly in danger from overfishing and pollution. Overfishing occurs when too many fish are caught in a particular fishing area. Numbers of both adult and young fish become dangerously low, and fewer fish survive to breed.

Scientists are trying to find ways to control overfishing. One way is for governments to set limits on the number of fish that can be caught in certain areas, or to prevent fishing during the breeding season. Another way is to use nets with a mesh big enough to allow younger fish to escape so they can go on to breed.

Many fish die or become diseased in polluted waters. Oil leaks from tankers, the pumping of sewage into the sea, and the dumping of chemical waste into fresh water are all causes of

This boat is spraying an oil slick to make it sink. Oil pollution is a danger to sea creatures and can ruin beaches.

water pollution. Even the chemicals used by farmers to improve their crops are eventually washed away into rivers and out to sea.

Shellfish

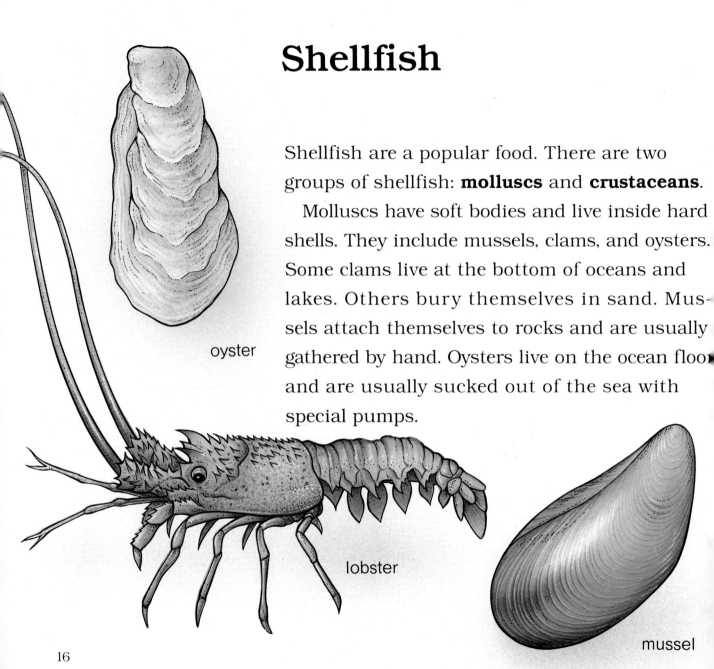

Shellfish are a popular food. There are two groups of shellfish: **molluscs** and **crustaceans**.

Molluscs have soft bodies and live inside hard shells. They include mussels, clams, and oysters. Some clams live at the bottom of oceans and lakes. Others bury themselves in sand. Mussels attach themselves to rocks and are usually gathered by hand. Oysters live on the ocean floor and are usually sucked out of the sea with special pumps.

oyster

lobster

mussel

You may be surprised to learn that the octopus and the squid belong to the mollusc family. In prehistoric times, they too had outer shells. They are usually caught in nets.

Crustaceans have a hard, shell-like covering that is actually an outer skeleton. They include crayfish, which live in fresh water, and saltwater shellfish such as crabs, lobsters, shrimp, and prawns. Crabs and lobsters are trapped in cages. Prawns and shrimp are caught in nets. Crayfish are trapped in special nets that are stretched over hoops.

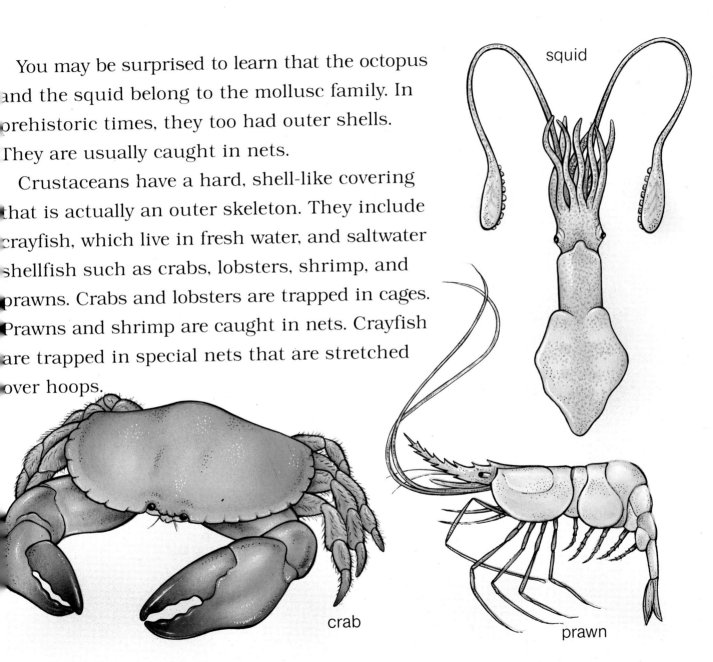

squid

crab

prawn

Freshwater fish and fish farming

Freshwater fish live in the salt-free waters of rivers, lakes, ponds, and streams. They include trout, perch, salmon, and carp. Freshwater fishing is a popular hobby.

Some freshwater fish are bred and kept in **fish farms**. Fish are raised in these farms for food and to restock rivers and lakes.

There are two methods of fish farming. In

Above: This bridge is used for trout fishing. The traps are used to catch eels.

Right: Trout and carp are often raised in freshwater fish farms.

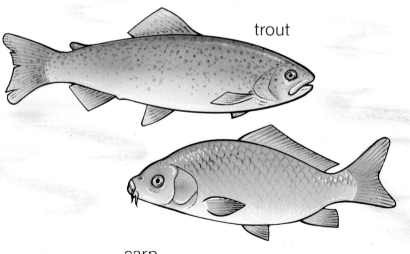

trout

carp

extensive farming, fish are raised in large, roomy ponds where they have a natural supply of food. For **intensive farming**, fish are crowded together in long, narrow ponds or circular tanks. Clean water flows through the ponds, and the farmer supplies food for the fish to eat. In farms, fish are protected from predators, pollution, and other harmful factors.

Some saltwater fish are farmed in a similar way, in farms set up in coastal waters.

The giant pools of this coastal fish farm in Israel look almost like farmlands.

From catch to store

Once fish are caught, the nets are hauled up onto the ship, and the catch is emptied out. Th[e] fish are then packed in ice and stored.

On big commercial ships, workers may also **gut**, clean, and **fillet** the fish. Large numbers of fish fillets may be deep-frozen together. These ships can stay at sea for months. Smaller ships.

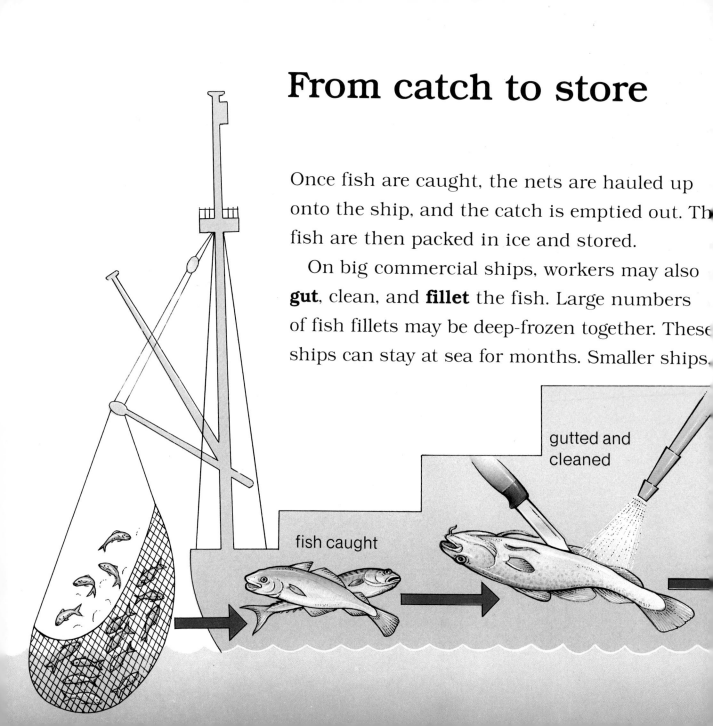

fish caught

gutted and cleaned

which cannot freeze their catch, must return to port quickly to sell their fish.

Fish are usually sold by auction at fish markets, but some fish are sold by contract. Buyers agree to buy the fish at a certain price before they are caught. The fish are then transported by train or truck in refrigerated containers to fish markets or factories. Factories use fish to make products such as fish sticks and fish cakes.

This diagram shows the various stages fish go through from the catch to the store.

filleted

deep-frozen

transported to markets or stores

Keeping fish fresh

Fish must be eaten when it is as fresh as possible, or it can make you very ill. Today, fish can be kept fresh for long periods of time by refrigeration. Keeping fish chilled in refrigerators slows the rate at which bacteria can increase. Fish can be frozen solid and stored until it is needed.

Fish may also be preserved by canning, drying

Octopuses are hung on a rack to dry on this Greek beach.

pickling, or smoking. An increasing number of fish are canned. These fish are cleaned and prepared, then cut up and packed into cans. The cans are made airtight, sealed, and heated. Heating kills bacteria and sealing the cans keeps new bacteria from entering. In the United States, one-fifth of all fish caught are canned.

Salting fish and smoking them over a smoldering fire of wood shavings and sawdust preserves them and gives them a distinctive taste that many people find delicious. Some fish are pickled in brine (salt water) or vinegar.

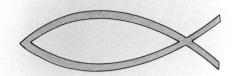

Beliefs about fish

Above: The sign of the fish, used by early Christians
Below: A fishing festival in Nigeria. Part of the river is closed off all year long, and perch are bred in it. On one special day each year, 1,000 men plunge into the river with their nets to catch the fish.

The sign of the fish once played an important part in the Christian religion. Early Christians were forbidden to follow their chosen religion and had to keep their faith a secret. By drawing a simple sign of a fish on walls or doors, they could show other Christians that they shared the same belief.

Many Roman Catholics eat fish, and no meat

Above: A fish seller sets out a display in his store. Some people believe it is wrong to kill living creatures for food.

on Fridays. This is in memory of Good Friday, which Christians believe is the day that Jesus Christ died to save humankind.

Many Buddhists and Hindus do not eat any fish or meat. They believe that it is wrong to cause suffering to living creatures by killing them for food. They are vegetarians and eat only plant and dairy products. Many people choose to be vegetarians, some for religious or health reasons, and some because they do not believe in killing animals for food.

Fish cakes

You will need:

12 oz. can salmon or tuna
¾ lb. potatoes, boiled and mashed
1 tablespoon chopped fresh parsley
1 oz. margarine   vegetable oil
salt and pepper   1 beaten egg
a little milk   ½ cup breadcrumbs

1. Open the can of fish and place contents in a mixing bowl. Mash with a fork.

2. Mix the fish with the potatoes, parsley, margarine, salt, and pepper. If the mixture does not hold together, add milk to bind.

3. On a floured surface, form the mixture into a roll and cut into eight slices. Shape into flat cakes.

4. Dip the cakes into the beaten egg and then into the breadcrumbs.

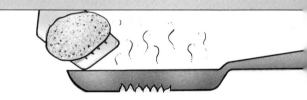

5. Heat the oil in a frying pan, add the fish cakes, and fry them. Turn once. When they are crisp and golden, drain them and serve. Be careful when frying!

Tuna-stuffed eggs

You will need, for 2 people:

4 eggs
2 tablespoons mayonnaise
salt and pepper
3 oz. of canned tuna fish
2 tomatoes, sliced
lettuce or fresh parsley

3. In a bowl, mash the yolks with a fork. Add the mayonnaise, salt, and pepper. Stir well.

4. Open the can of tuna, drain it, and mash the fish in a mixing bowl with a fork. Mix the fish with the egg mixture.

1. Boil the eggs for 10 minutes. Cool them down in cold water. Peel them carefully.

2. Cut the eggs in half and scoop out the yolks with a small spoon.

5. Spoon the mixture into each hollow egg white. Arrange the eggs on a serving plate. Use the tomatoes and lettuce or parsley as garnish.

Fish curry

You will need, for 3 people:
6 haddock fillets
3 tablespoons butter or margarine
1 onion, peeled and chopped
1 cooking apple, peeled and chopped
2-3 level teaspoons of curry powder
3 tablespoons flour
1 quart (32 oz.) chicken or fish stock
salt and pepper
1 teaspoon sugar
2 teaspoons chutney
¾ cup rice

Preheat the oven to 350°F.

1. Melt the butter in a frying pan. When it is melted, fry the onions for 5 minutes. Add the apple and fry for 2 more minutes. Then add the curry powder and fry for another 5 minutes.

2. Add the flour and stir the mixture. Gradually pour in the stock. Add salt, pepper, sugar, and chutney and stir.

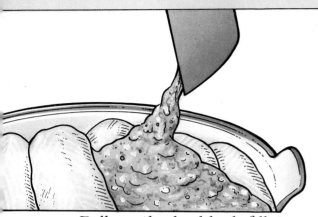

3. Roll up the haddock fillets. Place them in a casserole or ovenproof dish. Pour the sauce over the fish and cover the dish.

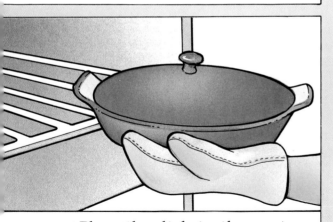

4. Place the dish in the center of the oven. Cook for 20-30 minutes and remove from the oven.

5. Serve on a bed of rice. Cook the rice in 1½ cups of boiling water for about 20 minutes. You will need to put the rice on to cook at about the same time as the fish goes into the oven.

Glossary

crustaceans: shellfish that are covered by a hard skeleton

extensive farming: raising fish in roomy areas with a natural food supply

fillet: to remove the bones from a fish

fisheries: areas where fish are caught

fish farms: areas of water where fish are bred and raised

gills: the membranes that fish breathe through

gut: to cut open a fish and remove its innards

intensive farming: raising fish in special ponds or tanks with a controlled food supply

molluscs: shellfish that have soft bodies and live inside hard shells

plankton: microscopic plants and animals that live in the ocean and are eaten by fish

purse-seine nets: fishing nets that are closed by pulling in lines at the bottom of the net

trawlers: fishing boats that catch fish by scooping them up in trawl nets

Index

Photo acknowledgments

The photographs in this book were provided by: pp. 6, 13, 15, 18, 23 (left), 24, J. Allan Cash; pp. 7, 19, 25, Hutchison Library; pp. 8, 9, 12, Wayland Picture Library; pp. 22, 23 (right), Christine Osborne.